The
Smallest
Muscle
in the
Human
Body

The
Smallest
Muscle
in the
Human
Body

ALBERTO RÍOS

COPPER CANYON PRESS

Printed in the United States of America.

Grateful acknowledgment is made to Fernando Botero for the use of his painting, *Still Life with Watermelon*, 1974, on the cover.

Copper Canyon Press is in residence under the auspices of the Centrum Foundation at Fort Worden State Park in Port Townsend, Washington. Centrum sponsors artist residencies, education workshops for Washington State students and teachers, Blues, Jazz, and Fiddle Tunes Festivals, classical music performances, and the Port Townsend Writers' Conference.

LIBRARY OF CONGRESS CATALOGING-IN-PUBLICATION DATA
Ríos, Alberto.
   The smallest muscle in the human body / by Alberto Ríos.
     p. cm.
   Includes bibliographical references.
   ISBN 1-55659-173-X (pbk. : alk. paper)
    1. Mexican-American Border Region—Poetry. 2. Hispanic Americans—Poetry. I. Title.
   PS3568.I587 S63 2002
   811'.54—dc21

                                    2001006505

9 8 7 6 5 4 3 2 second printing

COPPER CANYON PRESS
Post Office Box 271
Port Townsend, Washington 98368
www.coppercanyonpress.org

ACKNOWLEDGMENTS

These poems appeared in earlier versions in the following journals and books:

Artemis; Atlanta Review; Blue Mesa Review; Clackamas Literary Review; Cream City Review; Danger: Poets at Play; Hayden's Ferry Review; Indiana Review; Journal of Ethnic Studies; The Lucid Stone; Meridian; New Letters; North American Review; Otra Canción/Another Song: Seis Poetas Norteamericano; Pequod; Portlander; Prairie Schooner; Quarterly West; Revista Chicano Riqueña; Rio Grande Review; Seasons of the Coyote; Slant; Solo; South Carolina Review; Southwestern American Literature; Tampa Review; Texas Observer; and *The William and Mary Review.*

I want to thank the editors of these publications, the early readers of this collection, and Arizona State University.

CONTENTS

for Lupita

A PHYSICS OF SUDDEN LIGHT

This is just about light, how suddenly
One comes upon it sometimes and is surprised.

In light, something is lifted.
That is the property of light,

And in it one weighs less.
A broad and wide leap of light

Encountered suddenly, for a moment—
You are not where you were

But you have not moved. It's the moment
That startles you up out of dream,

But the other way around: It's the moment, instead,
That startles you into dream, makes you

Close your eyes—that kind of light, the moment
For which, in our language, we have only

The word *surprise,* maybe a few others,
But not enough. The moment is regular

As with all the things regular
At the closing of the twentieth century:

A knowledge that electricity exists
Somewhere inside the walls;

That tonight the moon in some fashion will come out;
That cold water is good to drink.

The way taste slows a thing
On its way into the body.

Light, widened and slowed, so much of it: It
Cannot be swallowed into the mouth of the eye,

Into the throat of the pupil, there is
So much of it. But we let it in anyway,

Something in us knowing
The appropriate mechanism, the moment's lever.

Light, the slow moment of everything fast.
Like hills, those slowest waves, light,

That slowest fire, all
Confusion, confusion here

One more part of clarity: In this light
You are not where you were but you have not moved.

ONE

DAY OF THE REFUGIOS

In Mexico and Latin America, it is common to celebrate one's saint's day
instead of one's birthday. This is an act of community.

I was born in Nogales, Arizona,
On the border between
Mexico and the United States.

The places in between places,
They are like little countries
Themselves, with their own holidays

Taken a little from everywhere.
My Fourth of July is from childhood,
Childhood itself a kind of country, too.

It's a place that's far from me now,
A place I'd like to visit again.
The Fourth of July takes me there.

In that childhood place and border place
The Fourth of July, like everything else,
It meant more than just one thing.

In the United States the Fourth of July,
It *was* the United States.
In Mexico it was the *día de los Refugios,*

The saint's day of people named Refugio.
I come from a family of people with names,
Real names, not-afraid names, with colors

Like the fireworks: Refugio,
Margarito, Matilde, Alvaro, Consuelo,
Humberto, Olga, Celina, Gilberto.

Names that take a moment to say,
Names you have to practice.
These were the names of saints, serious ones,

And it was right to take a moment with them.
I guess that's what my family thought.
The connection to saints was strong:

My grandmother's name—here it comes—
Her name was Refugio,
And my great-grandmother's name was Refugio,

And my mother-in-law's name, now,
It's another Refugio—Refugios everywhere,
Refugios and shrimp cocktails and sodas.

Fourth of July was a birthday party
For all the women in my family
Going way back, a party

For everything Mexico, where they came from,
For the other words and the green-tinted glasses
My great-grandmother wore.

These women were me,
What I was before me,
So that birthday fireworks in the evening,

All for them,
This seemed right.
In that way the fireworks were for me, too.

Still, we were in the United States now,
And the Fourth of July,
Well, it was the Fourth of July.

But just what that meant,
In this border place and time,
It was a matter of opinion in my family.

THE BIRDMAN OF NOGALES

The Birdman wasn't a bird
So much—he was a beaver, too,

With some horse and a flock of crows
Where the pupils of his eyes should have been.

He was a trapper in those years,
A prospector if he found a good rock.

Sometimes he was a sheep, just grazing,
Just out there, an off-white

Part of a regular landscape,
Except up close.

He had gathered to himself through the years
Something of everything he knew,

A little bit of what he touched, his eyes
In their sudden blink

Catching, if just a molecule, a moment
From the glint of a sharp piece of quartz.

He was some parts animal, some parts
Shiny, and some parts so thin

They had no echo or shadow or taste.
He was dressed by his parts,

They took hold of him,
So a little of him snarled when he walked.

The shiny parts lit his way,
The human told him to eat.

He came down from the low mountains
Around town, fall of every year.

That was when he wavered, when Nature
Itself wavered, in its leaves,

In the air, in the brown.
He came to town for coffee,

For sugar, and to think.
He had a ponytail.

This was not a ponytail from a flashy decade,
This was not a ponytail for show or for fashion.

It was more. The size and color of a forearm
Tattooed, with a mouth and two ears

In the right light,
It was a personal ponytail,

Something that lasted.
He had left it alone, uncombed,

Ragged, pulled together but only a little,
Only as much as he could after years.

It matted itself and made grease;
It had a low-order shine and a solid look,

The hairs more etched on than actually there.
From behind, the Birdman was another thing,

A beaver at the top,
A split river at the blue jeans of his legs.

He drank his coffee slowly
And he stayed always about a month.

You could count on him.
This much of him was a season, too.

He didn't talk much, but he smiled
After a while, after two weeks, or three.

It was a painful smile,
A little too much to the left.

Then somewhere in October, every time,
Some animal just came out of him.

It reached down with something like hands.
It pulled his pants a little higher,

Hard enough so we could see it.
Hard enough so that he had to get up.

He'd finish his coffee to the last,
But he felt it, too. He'd get up.

Then he would walk out, a little like a horse,
Until we couldn't see him.

Maybe he waved. Maybe
It was one of his large ears twitching.

He'd walk a line toward the hills, and go into them—
Into them, not over them.

THE WEEKLY MORNING MEETING OF THE TOWN'S CIVIC BAND

A hundred trombone players in a single-file line
Without any other instruments:

Things began here by someone starting a civic band,
Then choosing the trombone as his instrument.

Not wanting to be outdone or cheated,
The second one in line also chose a trombone,

And on things went. Because there was no leader,
Nobody could say this wouldn't work

And so there came to be a hundred of them,
Just like that, all trombones.

They'd start out with everyone sitting down in a room,
But this didn't work: like the instrument,

They began to slide out, out the door,
And as one went so did the others

Until they were in the street
Like a swarm of bees, sometimes

Like cattle with their low sounds,
But everybody in a single line

Because that is how they came out the door,
And so it was what they knew.

A hundred trombone players in a single-file line
The whole morning—this is the Trombone Club—

Wandering through public buildings, private backyards,
A snaking line, grizzled, untutored and sinewy,

All of them playing the same song—
Not the same way, but wanting the song

Right. They hold to a middle
But charm around it, like the ribs of a snake:

They are before the song, and after, above
The song, they echo and mute and slide it,

A hundred trombone players in a single-file line
Playing something—it's dangerous—

The hundred thousand things a single song is,
Released at once to an air that is full.

A SIMPLE THING TO KNOW

The whole thing is not much: A man
On the border between Douglas and Agua Prieta,

This man, on instructions from his wife—
For the family and because she couldn't,

He went shopping.
He crossed from Mexico to the United States,

Walking past the officials, who looked busy.
He didn't want to bother them

And he didn't want to wait.
He walked past them, just a little.

But a little bit is enough.
They caught him and put him in jail.

It was a nice jail, he said later.
He thought they fed you better, though.

He thought they gave you food.
The man had come shopping for some tuna.

He thought of it now.
They put him in the jail on a Thursday,

Then they forgot.
Nobody checked, nobody brought food.

He was so quiet
Nobody knew he was there.

It's a small jail.
The arresting officer forgot to tell the next shift.

On Saturday the janitor found the man
Sitting on his bench.

Why didn't you say something?
The man shrugged his shoulders.

The shrug said he was a good guest.
It said he knew how to behave.

It said the question was the wrong question.
Why didn't he say something?

This question was a trick.
The man would not be fooled.

The man had manners.
He knew going in what was right.

Speak only when spoken to.
And in jail, in jail especially.

It was a simple thing to know.

MR. PALOMINO WALKS BY AGAIN

I

Pointing a pickle finger at his mouth,
A scotch is welcome here,

He says, nodding his radish head
Hard, his thin body shaking with it.

It's welcome here because I drink,
It's what I do.

It's not like rakes or hammers,
Which don't make any difference in the world,

Not finally,
Not when everything falls down.

His insides, his mouth and his windpipe,
Visible from the outside as a skeleton's,

His mouth and windpipe
Hang to him, they hang to the outside of him.

They look like a young girl's arm and fist,
His mouth the bulb of her folded fingers

Flexing in some vague further mumble,
Opening and closing all the time

The way a boxer tests his hand,
The way circus fat ladies look,

Always chewing when they breathe:
Like fish, like that.

It's not a young girl's arm after all.
Nothing so big.

It's not what it used to be.
It's a mouth that is a baby's hand.

2

When he walks away he does not
Walk away: he stays, a leaning tower.

The wind will not help him stand,
It will not blow from the other side.

Its touch instead comes cruel like his wife's,
The wind's breath, her breath,

Both of them pushing the other way.
He cannot feel them anymore,

His skin having had to get thick
For that, thick against the push

Collected into one bully's shoulder
Whose face is different every time,

Pushing this folded man along
The street that comes back to here

In circles, toward no smell of cooking.
Mr. Palomino's arthritis, his rednesses,

His face: they shout back every time.
The lines in his face risen to color,

His horse skin and his hair bright with water:
This is his way to be strong.

But then, the colors moan in him the moan
Dogs sometimes let out of their sleep,

Battle song of the inside
Beast that can touch and not be touched.

Mr. Palomino points a pickle finger at his mouth
Then points it at me: *Please,*

He says, *a little,* to help him quiet
What he sees me looking at.

At the Street Parties for the
16 de Septiembre, Nogales, Mexico, 1962

Out of wires and scrap, someone would assemble
The head of a bull. Someone

Held on to it, or put it on, and tied to it
A string of a hundred red Chinese firecrackers

Linked by a lace of fuse.
The fireworks took the shape of a centipede

As I looked, my ten-year-old eyes
Seeing, in the web of fuses,

The legs of a centipede at work.
It was a writhing crown,

The legs of a centipede with the head of a bull.
The fuse would be lit the second it was done,

The assemblage in its tangle being anything—
The centipede for me, but the ribs of a rattlesnake

Or the contorting fingers of *el malo*
There, just as well, in the moment of fire.

The animals were there,
So the person would run through

The crowd, which squealed and was its own animal.
There were laughter and burns, a small drink of joy

And trampling—nothing in between—and gray smoke.
As the animals found their quiet,

I was not fooled.
The centipede had flown

On the rise of explosion,
Then found itself again.

I saw it through the years
Watching old Mr. Palomino smile.

In the line his teeth made as his jaws joined,
I saw the line of body his lips made:

There was the centipede, and its legs I could see:
They were those dark lines between his teeth.

LOS VOLADORES DE PAPANTLA

I saw the Flying Men of Papantla in the 1950s,
And then several times since,

The Tarascan Indians from inside Mexico
Playing flutes, some of them, the others answering

From the small platform at the top of a fifty-foot pole,
Binding their ankles to the end of a rope.

It was the first time that stays with me,
Especially now. Today it's neat and clean—

The ropes are checked and insurance forms are signed.
But the first time, people crowded right up to the pole

And the men jumped without testing first.
Their ropes, anyone could see, were homemade.

These men were not putting on a show.
They were painted but were not clowns.

Their ropes were like fuses
And their thin, reddened bodies

Like penny firecrackers.
They were faith-jumpers

And it was religion we were in the middle of,
Religion with silver sweat and with yellow screams,

Whole audiences in thrall to blood that was real.
These were fireworks, like any,

The explosions, the green
And the blue, the rosettes of sparkle

Imagined easily, so clear was the next moment:
A man would jump.

At that moment in life and in the world anything could happen.
People clasped their hands together

In prayer, but as much in desperation.
With so many crowded in, it just sounded like applause.

APPOINTMENT HOUSES

At the house of the bachelors,
The men in the garage keep their chairs in a circle
To account for the hours of afternoon.

They sit there, their lips and ears,
Their folds of leathery skin like petals,
Like wood violets which grow around the bases of trees.

They need a little protection,
But they're perennials and stay around
Once they've found a place.

The men are a little purple in the face
And a little red, with some brown
From the eyes, some brown and some white and white-yellow.

It's different from the old orange color
Of the women next door,
The orange and the deep red.

At the house of the widows
Who sit in their own garage,
Facing the men but across the fence,

The colors are different
And a little like dandelions sometimes,
Held on with so much powder.

If a good wind came, one of the men would start,
It would blow half of them over there away.
They died a long time ago.

They're just so old they forgot.
With that the men would laugh
And the women would turn their backs

And one of them would say, *Look.*
Look at that appointment house.
You know, they'd say,

That's what they used to call whorehouses
In the old days, casas de cita,
But now all their appointments are with doctors.

The men would shake their heads,
Every one in an *I'll-show-you.*
It was an old dance now,

Not a polka anymore, not the *norteño* rhythms
They had all grown up with.
It was ballet, these exchanges of words

Over the wire fence. A ballet,
A little, with some of the red theater
A good bullfight provides,

The charging animals of their words
All either side having left that would move.
They could turn in their chairs

And make faces, elegant—like matadors
With that exquisite and heated slowness—
But their slowness was from pain now,

Not that old dishrag, Desire.
The slowness now could look like that something else,
But it was pain.

Because of this, the game did not last very long.
The game was short,
It was like childhood.

But they got a taste when they had a good word
In the mouth.
They got a taste of childhood in the word,

And when they said their word, whatever it was—
It was new each time,
Even after so many years—

It was like spraying out watermelon seeds and juice
All over everyone.
To make a joke or to construct a good insult,

Built with the bricks of the old days,
Then to pass it over the fence,
This was the game of tag.

It was tag and marriage and sex and infidelity
And all the rest.
Nobody said *You're it,* because the phrase was so much inside them,

Inside the memory in their legs:
You're it, their legs would say,
And then they would run as fast and as far as they could.

KID HIELERO

He had a couple of fights
But they didn't add up.

Kid Hielero became a name for the bars,
A name for a laugh,

As if who could believe it
Looking at him later,

Or it was just a name to remember,
The way one talked about radio shows,

The Shadow, and who could remember
The man's real name, Lamont Cranston—

As if a radio guy could have a real name.
But it's what we said anyway,

And didn't think about it.
Anyone from Nogales in the fifties

Would remember it—
Well they'd remember it, but maybe not him:

Kid Hielero took his name
From the old icehouse

Right on Grand Avenue, coming in—
The *hielero,* where he worked for a while

The way everyone worked for a while
At some point in life.

Small towns work like this.
The ice chutes used to pass over

The road through town
And ice water dripped like rain

Onto the cars underneath.
It could have been a car wash

And everybody could have been rich—
But it wasn't, and they weren't.

These were the days when the railroad
Needed ice

For the cabbages and the lettuce,
The masses of sugar beets.

It was in the days when small towns,
You know what I mean,

Needed themselves.
Kid Hielero died

In another time altogether,
Suffering the invention of cancer.

When it happened
All he wanted was watermelon.

It was a fancy hospital
And the nurses got some

Even though it was winter, September.
I remember they said they were ready

For this. They said,
Somebody who's dying,

They always want watermelon.
It's the women from Mexico

In the kitchen, they knew
Right from the beginning

This would happen.
Not for him, of course, not specifically,

Just for people like him.
So they freeze a little in the summer.

The nurses said the women in the kitchen said
It's from another time

And it's all I could say, too:
Yes, I said.

I think that's true,
It's from another time.

I think that's what you say,
And I think it helps.

Kid Hielero watched the World Series
And ate the watermelon

And died,
And he left me his daughter

For a wife.
It happened quickly

So that everyone forgot
About the watermelon,

Just like The Shadow's real name.
But there it is

And I don't know what you do with it.
You remember it sometimes.

That's all you can do.
Remember it and think about it,

Because there you are with it
Every time you eat watermelon.

REFUGIO'S HAIR

In the old days of our family,
My grandmother was a young woman
Whose hair was as long as the river.
She lived with her sisters on the ranch
La Calera—The Land of the Lime—
And her days were happy.

But her uncle Carlos lived there too,
Carlos whose soul had the edge of a knife.
One day, to teach her to ride a horse,
He made her climb on the fastest one,
Bareback, and sit there
As he held its long face in his arms.

And then he did the unspeakable deed
For which he would always be remembered:
He called for the handsome baby Pirrín
And he placed the child in her arms.
With that picture of a Madonna on horseback
He slapped the shank of the horse's rear leg.

The horse did what a horse must,
Racing full toward the bright horizon.
But first he ran under the *álamo* trees
To rid his back of this unfair weight:
This woman full of tears
And this baby full of love.

When they reached the trees and went under,
Her hair, which had trailed her,
Equal in its magnificence to the tail of the horse,
That hair rose up and flew into the branches
As if it were a thousand arms,
All of them trying to save her.

The horse ran off and left her,
The baby still in her arms,
The two of them hanging from her hair.
The baby looked only at her
And did not cry, so steady was her cradle.
Her sisters came running to save them.

But the hair would not let go.
From its fear it held on and had to be cut,
All of it, from her head.
From that day on, my grandmother
Wore her hair short like a scream,
But it was long like a river in her sleep.

TWO

Small Risings

The middle summer light in water
Coming through the rain and window
Makes new shadows on me,
Giving me appendages I had not seen—
A second nose,
A sixth finger.
They were no surprise.
I had suspected them and others
Since childhood,
Having seen, if I moved my wrist quickly,
Ten or twelve fingers on a single hand.
Two noses every day, one on my face,
One in the mirror. I could touch
Each to each in a meeting of nostrils,
All four of them clearly mine.
The rain and its afternoon shadows
Give me what I already know.
Sometimes at night I get up
And from my bed I watch myself,
My other legs, the rising back of my head,
The tired intent to brush my hair.
I see myself go, that me
When I walk out the door.

SIGNAL RIGHT

When the car breaks down,
The world goes wrong:

Something suddenly
Makes right

Signals by hand from a Ford,
Something from the old days,

Something from getting things done
The way they'd always been done,

The way that works again.
How could we not remember this?

The wild riding of a spotted horse,
One hand tied

To the horn of its saddle,
The other hand up, waving

Then jackhammered,
The fingers of this second hand

Spread out, windmill-like,
This second hand, this third hand—

The way a hand can look like so many—
Moving fast, the fingers

Spread out strong.
The fingers, too, they are a hundred

Fingers in that blur,
The hundred

Real fingers hidden
In every hand,

Every hand that tries
To point oneself from here

To where it is
We want to go.

FRENCH POSTALES

That darkness of night,
We think about it.

When we think about it,
Night becomes anything:

The opening a man gives of his coat
Somewhere, someplace foreign—

Which is to say, it can't happen here—
As he tries to show us French postcards,

The curious man keeping his coat
A little to himself and a little to us.

He needs a darkness for his work,
For his place in the world.

But what he shows us in there, in the pockets,
In the recesses of fabric in his coat,

In his night: The stars,
They are the French postcards

And they are just what we think—
Nudes upon nudes,

Which is to say, nothing
But nudity, and nudity

Inside there is everything. Nothing but body,
Bones, skin. But on fire.

Marrow lit up
At the end of a bone

Grasped as a torch.
Did you think I had not meant

Men as well?
They hang in some order, these cards,

An order we recognize,
Two upon one, four upon two,

A family tree
Of desires and of dares.

In the darkness of his coat there is nudity,
But the darkness lasts only a moment,

Until our eyes adjust. Then
The nakedness lights everything up.

The light moves from the inside of his coat
To inside us, somehow: It is a magnetism

Between light and dark, a full balance,
The way water fills a crevice.

In his darkness, his stars,
We think about them. The stars in the sky:

Who could have supposed they were fruit
Like they are, the other stars,

Fruit up in the sky, in the night,
The pears and the apples, persimmons.

This is the fruit that does not fall,
The fruit we think we never see

But which is the harvest
That comes from looking up, looking

But not looking at the sky. The way
It hypnotizes us into just thinking.

All of this is not difficult to see.
It is the empty, clean space

On a dinner plate, the place
Where apples have been, the place

Where nectarines will be,
And summer oranges and wild berries.

They are appetite, magnetic cousin to desire.
Fruit, as substantial as it feels

In the mouth,
It is just metaphor.

The postcards the man shows us,
Well, it's nothing we haven't seen

Somewhere in the night, in the sky,
In the stars, the millionfold stars

Which come down to be our dinner plates,
To hold for us everything we put upon them.

In Second Grade Miss Lee I Promised Never to Forget You and I Never Did

In a letting-go moment
Miss Lee the Teacher
Who was not married
And who the next year was not at school,
Said to us, her second grade,
French lovers in the morning
Keep an apple next to the bed,
Each taking a bite
On first waking, to take away
The blackish breath of the night,
You know the kind.
A bite and then kissing,
And kissing like that was better.

I saw her once more
When she came to sell encyclopedias.
I was always her favorite—
The erasers, and the way she looked at me.
I promised, but not to her face,
Never to forget
The story of the apples.
Miss Lee all blond hair and thin,
Like *a real movie star*
If she would have just combed herself more.
Miss Lee, I promised,
I would keep apples
For you.

EATING POTATO CHIPS IN MIDDLE AGE

When I eat a salty potato chip, now,
I'm wild and do not waste

What is crisp, I taste it
And chew it to a crinkled knot.

I taste and lisp out
Nothing. I keep it all and keep it

In, I let it go
Out in songs, the breath toward

Music, the tendons toward dance, that
Gorging, that coming back. I'm saying,

I eat what I like
Sometimes, wrong and right and watery.

Salt, in the mouth, salt:
The mouth thinking it

Makes water, that horse
Potato chip kicking, hooves and shoes

Hard against the stall, the walls
The mouth has: Something there cries,

But from good: a potato chip.
Think it, and in the mouth something happens.

The Venus Trombones

If my legs were my arms
And my eyes were elbows,
If my hips were my palms
And my hair was made of fingers,
Nothing would work

At first. But if
My legs grew thicker,
If my elbows started to see,
If my hips got their feel back
And my fingers combed themselves,

But if, before that, my legs weren't my arms
At all—it's just that the names for things,
The names got changed
In one of those legislative bills
By a first-year senator,
So that my legs stayed my legs
But were now called my *arms,*
Eyes were *elbows* and *hips* were *palms,*

What then? Nothing changed
And everything changed.
Which the stronger? The names for things,
The things themselves?
Which the stronger, *yesterday*
Or *today? Today* or *tomorrow?*

The first answers may be as tedious
As these first questions, until
These names are changed, too—
Questions become *potatoes,*
Answers become *blood.*
Not so easy, then, to pair
Questions and answers
So quickly, so immediately.

And a person without eyes, a person
Without legs, without an arm, taken
In the explosions—the *cockroach*—
We created and gifted to one another
In packages on which gift cards read:
World Love II and *The Vietnam Love*—
Is this person more or less?

The answers—the *puddings*—are out there,
Are everywhere, are on us and in us,
Are in our dreams,
None of which makes sense.
We know this:
We do not understand our dreams.
Is that the fault of our dreams?
Is there a language—a *baby*—
We do not yet know?

Give the *Venus trombones* to the *salt*.
Pardon the *trucks* in my *hammer*.

MY CHILI

*The Santa Cruz River Valley lies a few miles north of the border between
Arizona and Sonora, Mexico, and it is marked by the Mission of San José de
Tumacácori, founded by Jesuits in the seventeenth century. The chilies that
come from there don't let you forget.*

Chili: First cousin to the ant bite,
Who, when in the mouth, talks about

This very cousin,
Talks slowly and spends a little time

Telling stories.
Chili, whose musical skin holds sound

Inside, the echoes from gold miners
In a heat, who used dynamite

To get at the veins of the gold.
That sound and that feeling,

A mustard impatience spurred on by dream.
Chili: All the times

I have shouted at you, not so many,
So that I remember them,

Something coming alive enough
And moving in the mouth

So that my body had no choice
And like hair had to spit it out:

This moment like the four times
In my life

I cut my feet
Walking on something, but so that

I shook them first. That kind of cut,
The kind that first seems like something else,

Like something clinging to the foot:
A nail once, and then

Something in the sand of the seawater
In Mexico that summer, that summer

Filled with jellyfishes, too,
That stung.

Chili: Witches' tongues,
Red and green and their darker

Familiars, *tongues,* where witches
Carry the seed of their kind,

Explaining their obsession for words
In spells, those hard rhyming words,

Wool coats to their children
In those tongues.

Chili taste: On a bar graph, distinctly
Between a fingersnap and a pinprick

But holding hands with both of them.
Walking calmly but realizing, in that same moment,

A bird dropping has fallen in your hair.
Opening the mailbox

To find the letter you have been waiting for
Is not there, again.

Chili taste: The feel of a counterfeit wound.
The sound of a whistle.

The sight of that other boy,
When he was young and you were young

And she was young, and she was with him.
It was a Thursday.

Chili: The small letter z
Which sometimes masquerades as the capital X,

Adding, thereby, to the other's reputation
Among the adults of the alphabet,

But chili content as z not to say anything,
Only to get the chance to live

Part of two lives.
Chili: Itself

And, at the crucial moment,
Also you.

It has taken you by the mouth
With its single muscle

And hit you, but from the inside out—
You can see the moment, which looks like

A tongue extending the cheek out.
Chili: The inside of a fist,

A fist's dream and a fist's intent.
It is the inside of a fight,

What you cannot see
But what is there.

Chili has begun.
It has already gone very far

Inside itself.
The moment you bite

You are saved the walk,
For plot purposes.

Instead you are leapt
To the place where chili is.

In a movie you are a detective.
You walk into a storefront

With a flashing red-and-green neon sign.
But as you step in

The floor suddenly gives out
From under you:

It is a trapdoor, and you fall
Down a two-story chute

To an immediately more interesting
Adventure in which you must remember

To hope
You are the hero.

Chili is a rapist or a lover.
What is important to recognize

Is that when one bites a chili
There is an unrecognized moisture

Suddenly in the mouth
And in the eyes, and sometimes on the skin.

It seems to have come from nowhere,
But that's not true.

If there were a hypnotist for the body
And not just the mind,

The body remembering, under oath
On the stand,

Would know where to point its finger—
Over there: That's the one who did it.

Then the chili would later have its photograph taken
At the police station

Or in the bedroom,
Left and right profiles and straight-on.

In the bedroom poses, in that intimacy,
Things would be just as we imagine

With a camera: That fascination—chili
With its legs just a little apart.

When you bite chili,
You are not biting chili.

With its own teeth and its own tongue
For taste,

The chili, after all,
Is biting you.

THREE

In My Hurry

The curious lavender attentions to itself of the jacaranda
Stopped me, as through the leaves and small avenues

In late summer I made my way in love toward you.
The tree's flowering was an intimacy I had not earned,

A color of undergarment or something from the better
Pages in the book already underlined by classmates.

It was lavender or lilac, something from the hundred blues,
This color without rank and without help, standing there,

Giving me the gift over and again but high up, outside
My reach, which made my desire to touch it all the more.

The color and the tree, the moment and the lateness of the season,
They joined in a gang of what I could see was a tangle of sinew,

So much muscle in search of the cover-skin of an arm,
The tree itself sceming all at once an arm unleashed,

Strength itself gone wild in its parts to the sky.
This was an arm that had stopped me—

How could I not have seen it? This tree was an arm
And more than arm, its muscle strung in everything

So that the tree—everything about it—the tree
Made itself of arm and leg, leg and neck, at angles,

At stops and starts and in bends, everything broken,
Everything but the lavender, which was flower,

So much lavender coming from what was left, what must be
A mouth, a thousand mouths, at once speaking

The lavender or the lilac, the blue, understood language.
These were match-tipped words asking the impossible of me,

Whatever I imagined the impossible to be: a bowl of cherries
In winter, or that I might come again by this place and stop.

Absent of reason, I could agree to anything addressing a tree.
The cherries were not much, I know, but what they meant,

Born of this exotic, all lavender and muscle, held me.
It was an equal and other necessity, calling to me in my hurry.

It was a tree in wild color calling to a tree in wild color,
And the lavender, I think you know what the lavender is.

THE NIPPLEBUTTON

1

I drew your nipple through a buttonhole,
Idly at first and then with purpose,

The intrigue of a nipplebutton
Suddenly discovered,

But in front of me all these years.
It doesn't hold, finally,

Not after some time
And the fuss of it all.

The blouse or the sweater
Opens up. But the idea persists,

And sometimes in a sudden moment I see it all
Make sense, the idea

So plain I could touch it.
But the light changes and the mind clears.

What might have been an impulse softens
And I say nothing.

2

As you sighed, I was drinking
A glass of ice water.

It was a long sigh
And I took it in as the glass of cold water.

The sigh came through the phone as we spoke
And went a long way into me:

I heard it in the same moment I drank the water—
In that moment it confused itself and became the water.

I felt it enter and slowly fall down, through me,
Doing what a glass of water will.

It was not conversation I drank down
But the lack of it,

The way water is not tea
And not chocolate

But something.
I drank down what you had no words for

And I felt it, the sigh-water,
I felt it move inside me.

A SMALL MOTOR

The easiest sadness is a boy
Watching another boy
Walk with a barefooted girl, clean

Perfect feet, that kind of nose,
Eyes like those he's dreamed
In the dream that comes back.

A boy watching another boy lucky
Gets an ache
That is a small motor.

In me there is an animal,
And in that animal
There is a hunger.

I remember the boy
Watching a boy.
It was me.

Watching, I was a little bit
The boy walking.
I was both of us.

That's how it felt.
What I could not have,
That's what I was

Inside, an ache
Coming as I stood
Too many places.

THE CITIES INSIDE US

We live in secret cities
And we travel unmapped roads.

We speak words between us that we recognize
But which cannot be looked up.

They are our words.
They come from very far inside our mouths.

You and I, we are the secret citizens of the city
Inside us, and inside us

There go all the cars we have driven
And seen, there are all the people

We know and have known, there
Are all the places that are

But which used to be, as well. This is where
They went. They did not disappear.

We each take a piece
Through the eye and through the ear.

It's loud inside us, in here, and when we speak
To the outside world

We have to hope that some of that sound
Does not come out, that an arm

Does not reach out
In place of the tongue.

WHAT WE'VE DONE TO EACH OTHER

There is a measure that maps don't get—
The up and the down of things.

From here to there is all right and plain
Enough, two steps to this place, nine steps

To the edge. I see the elevation lines,
Of course. But they don't look like Gold Hill.

I know. I've been there. On a map, the lines,
They look more like wrinkles on a knuckle.

But a hill is not made of lines. It's dirt there.
I know what I'm talking about.

Though, to be fair, I can see that when I fold my fingers
My knuckles do become little hills.

Looking at the scale of the map: The hair
Around my knuckles, this would be a small forest.

It's what you are supposed to believe:
One inch equals one mile. Just like that.

I'm saying, there is no wet on a map, only *ocean*
And *sea; river, lake,* some more words about water.

The word *lagoon* is there, but without any laughter
At having put that word in the mouth. *Lagoon.*

The map says *water,* but doesn't say it
Differently or oppositely from *land.*

The map of you is like this, all lines, all
Words. So is the great, folded map of me.

All wrinkles. That's the map of us
The world gets, and then believes:

We are what the map is supposed to do.
We are the up and the down of things,

But a map has the folds drawn on, and easy enough.
Ours are earned and not flat at all.

You can feel them. It's us, pushed down
In every one of those lines.

Our map is flat, but only to the eye.
We are the inside of the lines of the map.

We have folded ourselves into something: a real
Word, wetter than this map's *water*.

The map is everywhere on us.
You and I, that's what we've done to each other.

You can't believe the lines on a map,
But the lines on me,

They're what a map wants to say and can't.
We have made ourselves into where we want

To be, folded ourselves up
In our knees and our knuckles, our necks,

The lines beneath your eyes,
Everywhere in the fold of my elbows.

One inch equals one mile: I believe it.
That is us: In our arms, held out,

Some days just coming home, just tired,
Our arms held out toward each other.

One inch equals one mile: I believe it.
It would not be the first time I have seen such a thing.

FOUR

THE IMPOSSIBLE STILL-LIFE

A horse, as it stands along a ridge,
Looked-at against the sun
Rising above you, the light
Making a pure, thick, coloring-book line
Between sky and mountain—

That horse,
Loped back and with peaked ears,
A fine side rise and lift of neck,
The hillock of a nostril:

A horse, looked-at against the sun
In this way, becomes larger.
You see more of it. The whole thing

May be a trick of perspective,
Seeing in this place

The sudden angle of beginning.

Oranges in a Tree

1

The oranges in a tree won't fly away
If you're quiet. If you're quiet
You can see them in their nests—
Loud in the song of their great need,
Mouths tethered to the green beaks
That feed them, hushing their cries,
Pushing their infant noises into color,
That unmistakable sound, orange.

If you make noise, enough of a noise
And not just anything, a noise equal to theirs,
The oranges take flight
In a spin of movement that's dizzying
But which takes weeks.
Some fall to the ground in the excitement,
Falling from the fear of what you've said.
So many fall this way.

2

But some escape. Some move up,
Racing, onto the avenue of the birds,
Speeding at first, unruly and desperate
To get away. You can't see them,
They're so fast. You can't see them
Until they slow down, these oranges
In the air. They use up their color as food,
Finding places to hide, but they are plain enough

In a new rabbit's eyes, in the faraway
Lights of small towns, in falling stars, in the contrails
In the sky, in sudden sounds, orange sounds.
But those that land inside us, those that find their stopping point
Just where we stand: Those we feel
As flight inside ourselves, as the moment
We leave—how hard it is!—
The place where we had been.

3

As human beings,
We have a long history with birds.
We have eaten them as chickens and pigeons,
Doves and turkeys. We have caged them for amusement,
Made them fight each other for sport.
We have imitated their whistles and used up
The magic in their feathers.
After centuries, some birds have given themselves up

To this fate: They huddle themselves
Tightly as they can into anything but what they are—
They began to look like oranges and grapefruit,
Melons and squash. These were the birds
Who gave up flight, who gave up the air and the wandering.
Scientists have traced oranges back to oranges.
They did not know
To look for wings in the folds of the white rind.

A Yellow Leaf

A yellow leaf in the branches
Of a shamel ash
In the front yard:
I see it, a yellow leaf
Among so many.
Nothing distinguishes it,
Nothing striking, striped, stripped,
Strident, nothing
More than its yellow
On this day,
Which is enough, which makes me
Think of it later in the day,
Remember it in conversation
With a friend,
Though I do not mention it—
A yellow leaf on a shamel ash
On a clear day
In an Arizona winter,
A January like so many.

THE FALL OF THE BEARS

The bears have come to see what we have
For them. It is fall and easy enough
To walk on our trails, to stir themselves
One last time before winter.
Their noses read the newspapers of the wind.
It's the ads for the diners: They want
What we want—good water, pastries,
Bacon for breakfast
When we can get away with it.

The bears have come to see what we know
That they don't, like anybody would
Who sees a crowd gather. *What's happening
Over there?* we would ask, and we'd walk over
To take a look. I have done it many times.

The bears have come out of their hidden canyons
Around Phoenix, bears that walk like dogs,
Desert bears in the year of the fires,
These young bears loping into the early evening
Covered with creosote and cardboard boxes
Looking for a better life. They want jobs,
They want affordable housing, they want
What the city has. Who knew
The bears were so smart? Who knew
Their language was our language?

The bears grunt when we chase them,
They pant when they run, they thin
Themselves into the brush, black and invisible
At night. They startle when they hear us,
They try to get out of the way. They become
The barrel cactus. They become the trash can.
They do the things they will later tell
The grandchildren. *And it's all true,*
They will say, but it will be hard to believe them.

The bears sigh hard when we catch them, fall
To the ground in an early hibernation.
What happens afterward will be their winter dream,
Too early, the flying and the voices,
The hunger as big as a bear.

And when they wake it will be spring,
But no spring they have ever seen.
It will look like winter, which will look
Like the desert. It will smell like confusion.
It will feel like something is wrong.
They will start to look harder for home.

THE GATHERING EVENING

Shadows are the patient apprentices of everything.
They follow what might be followed,

Sit with what will not move.
They take notes all day long—

We don't pay attention, we don't see
The dark writing of the pencil, the black notebook.

Sometimes, if you are watching carefully,
A shadow will move. You will turn to see

What has made it move, but nothing.
The shadows transcribe all night.

Transcription is their sleep.
We mistake night as a setting of the sun:

Night is all of them comparing notes,
So many gathering that their crowd

Makes the darkness everything.
Patient, patient, quiet and still.

One day they will have learned it all.
One day they will step out, in front,

And we will follow them, be their shadows,
And work for our turn—

The centuries it takes
To learn what waiting has to teach.

GRAY DOGS

In the first early morning
Citrus light of summer, in blossoms
The happy dogs go running,
Becoming quickly indistinct
In the watery distance:
At the far reaches of the eye
They are two thin blurs
On a high desert canvas.
At this distance
They become thin.
They move quicker.
In the grasses and creosote
Their legs get lost—
The now-gray dogs have no legs.
They become ground-birds.
Their leaps become flight.
In the trick of distance
They fly into the trees.
They float over the streets
Made by branches.
The leaves hide their legs now,
The leaves and the light behind them.

All my dogs have died this way.
Beloved, beloved,
I see you now as I watch these two,
As I watch but cannot see them.
Gray dogs, all of you—
I see you running, but which is which?
Dogs flying in the trees,
Dogs in the clouds,
My gray dogs, my handsome dogs,
All of you, alive for a moment in the distance.
Two of them—the same two, I think—
Two dogs come running back to me
Finally, responding to my hoarse attentions.
They come back to tell me,

They nudge me and push,
They speak a language I know but don't
Think twice about, the barking
Details of a big story.
They are full of sweat and look hard at me,
My gray dogs, my gray dogs, back to color.
We walk toward home, but they try
Pulling me toward the trees.

Common Crows in a Winter Tree

The birds, they make this happen.
In the sky with nothing else to do, a Saturday,
The slow knee-bend of an afternoon, out there.

I have seen them myself.
The birds *caw* down a rain, tease it
To a hard ground of grass and flat and edge.

The birds, they cannot stop—they are birds.
They play when they do it. They don't mean it
When the rain reaches bottom.

But there is so much rain, and it listens
So well. Who would not, like the birds,
Try other things, try to train this water

To tricks, and to laughter? Circus
Ringmaster to a thousand lions of water:
Rain do this: And again: And now this.

To get away from the birds, the rain tries a mask:
It becomes snow, a show of wings, the flakes
Drunk moths in an aimless, cool wander.

Then it is ice, a trick again, rain

Turning into tiny fists without skin.
Hailstones, each a clutch of finger-bones,
Brittle, as much dry as wet. Rain to snow,

Then ice, then bone. Then more,
To skulls, and teeth, breaking against the earth
In a white fireworks of cruelty.

The birds, they get carried away, they cannot
Do a small thing or make a quiet noise.
But the birds do not mean it, this

Teasing of the sky to tears. They are birds—
They *caw* at anything, at little boys
Walking, boys who will look up.

And a loud *caw,* it will draw the boys, lift them
A little, until they cry. The birds
Do not mean to frighten,

But neither do they mean not to frighten,
Not to lift a boy into a branch
The way boys will go, lift a boy to a second

Branch, higher. The boys will go.
They cry at first, but they rise.
They are boys, and these are birds.

And the rain is falling. It makes a sound
Until snow, which is itself a sound,
Bigger and smaller than the moment before.

The boys come down from climbing, the boys who were lifted
Into trees, the boys who were birds.
The birds make their noise again, at something else.

My Coyote

It is not a dog, but a dog
Exponentially, a dog

Taken to the third power,
The algebraic dog

Made entirely of those parts
We do not want to think about:

Grizzly beast-hound of dream
Then, this indefatigable and licking

Walking rug, roof-carpet,
Carpet that will not stay

Where it belongs, lifeless and there.
It is instead a marvel carpet,

Moving so fast it seems to be flying,
Arabian in that way

We think of carpets from childhood,
From books and the inside-out of sleep,

Laughing riders in flight.
And this explains the sway

The coyote's back holds sure,
Its swoop and skulking horseback,

A generous and oversize saddle
Holding that invisible whoever-whatever

That spurs the coyote forward,
But unhappily and unsure,

Forward but bent,
Making the coyote's mouth hard,

Making a smile
Where there is no smile,

This smile
A trick of its markings.

So there we are again:
Coyote, trickster in its mask,

Trying to please the trickster
That rides it,

Magic upon magic,
A ladder of tricks.

That way we please
The trickster upon us,

The grizzly beast-hound of dream
That makes us laugh,

That makes us look like we laugh,
Our own mouths drawn

From the weight of what we bear.
But bear is another beast

So let us not start.
It is a dog

And not a dog.
Coyote, being tricked

And the trickster, too.
Coyote, like all of us.

What Happened to Me

A boy rides a horse after school
On a warm day and clear,
And on one day he does not hear
The call, one day does not come home.
The day is not less usual,
Not different from any other,
That particular day when now his mother
Cannot coolly bathe him, or comb him,
Or kiss his face, his hands, cannot
Fool this boy so easily about things.
The day is not different when he brings
Home nothing, though his hands are full.
On a warm day and clear
A boy rides a horse after school.
He is a small boy, still,
But the horse is big.
The world is there and this
Is its animal, and this,
His stepping off, is the getting on
The horse of the ground that will take him.

UNDER MESQUITE TREES IN THE SUN

Late summer water
Falls from the mesquites—
It is not water but water
Mixed with what it brings
From the leaves,
Water and silver
Raining in a dim-yellow light
Made thick from old blossoms
In the last of the afternoon, the heat
Being pushed to the ground,
Wrestled onto its animal back
But coming up from the raindrops—
Through the raindrops—
Not as splash but as steam.

RABBITS AND FIRE

Everything's been said
But one last thing about the desert,
And it's awful: During brush fires in the Sonoran desert,
Brush fires that happen before the monsoon and in the great,
Deep, wide, and smothering heat of the hottest months,
The longest months,
The hypnotic, immeasurable lulls of August and July—
During these summer fires, jackrabbits—
Jackrabbits and everything else
That lives in the brush of the rolling hills,
But jackrabbits especially—
Jackrabbits can get caught in the flames,
No matter how fast and big and strong and sleek they are.
And when they're caught,
Cornered in and against the thick
Trunks and thin spines of the cactus,
When they can't back up any more,
When they can't move, the flame—
It touches them,
And their fur catches fire.
Of course, they run away from the flame,
Finding movement even when there is none to be found,
Jumping big and high over the wave of fire, or backing
Even harder through the impenetrable
Tangle of hardened saguaro
And prickly pear and cholla and barrel,
But whichever way they find,
What happens is what happens: They catch fire
And then bring the fire with them when they run.
They don't know they're on fire at first,
Running so fast as to make the fire
Shoot like rocket engines and smoke behind them,
But then the rabbits tire
And the fire catches up,
Stuck onto them like the needles of the cactus,

Which at first must be what they think they feel on their skins.
They've felt this before, every rabbit.
But this time the feeling keeps on.
And of course, they ignite the brush and dried weeds
All over again, making more fire, all around them.
I'm sorry for the rabbits.
And I'm sorry for us
To know this.

The Dog inside Mine

The dog barks
Or is barked
By something inside,
Some mechanism in him
Taking hold
Against his best efforts
At sleep
Or civility.

The dog barks
Or is barked
By the dogs inside
The dark of him,
The black in his eyes,
The depths of his mouth,
Something from in there,
The growl of all
His mothers,
Like a hand,
Rousing his throat
Into noise.

This noise takes notice.
Or something has taken notice
And this noise
Is its charm:

It is not this dog's ears that hear.
It is the centuries,
And they answer back.

FIVE

CHINESE FOOD IN THE FIFTIES

There was only one place.
Kin Wah's, Nogales, Mexico.

I ate only the white rice.
I did not yet have the adventure in me

More than the name of this place,
The sight of a kind of food

Different from home.
Birds flew around me—

There were birds in this place,
In a cage from the floor to the ceiling,

Twenty birds or thirty birds, something
Adding from them to the taste of the food:

Their condiment sounds,
Something grainy from their voices

And their wings. Their noise made my white rice
Loud, though it was already a good taste

More than anyone could see.
But a spoon to the mouth, a *caw* to the ear—

This salt and ginger, an oil heated
And a scent rising, water making in the mouth—

It made me happy, this place and this food
Tasting like the voices of birds,

Each kernel of rice speaking in earnest
One parrot thing to the blue-winged next.

My parents would shrug to the waiter,
It's all he will eat.

It's all they could see,
The white rice, the almost

Whiteness between the rice, so much
White it seemed like nothing.

The waiter would laugh.
I hear it now, his laugh and the birds,

The faces of my parents twisted enough
To be themselves loud.

Their faces looked angry
The way the rice looked plain.

Neither one was the truth.
It was the fifties along the border.

They always asked me if I wanted something more.
But it was not the white rice

Filling me, making the fibers of a little boy.
The place filled me,

The way it was filled
With green and blue,

So that the white of the rice,
It was respite, a singular treat

In this place, stuffed like a pillow
With feathers wafting, filled with Chinese

Writing, the rice itself with its little sticks
Spelling something out, something

Bird. Something from flight.
Something from so much movement

It just looked like nothing. Wings,
The way the wings from birds,

From hummingbirds and bees,
From June bugs, the way in their moving wings

One sees nothing.
This was the place that was me

Filled with cage and with grit,
Filled with linoleum and with smoke.

This was the food that was me,
White rice. Nothing more.

SUMMERS, ABOUT 1959

Women wore those sleeveless blouses
Where, if you tried, you could peek in
And try to get a look.

But it was always the wrong angle.
Contact lenses got invented in those years, too.
I remember the first boy who got some:

He had big white lines
From his nose to his ears
As if he were wearing invisible glasses.

That's how someone explained them to me
And I believed it: invisible glasses.
But they were really just the tan lines

From so many years of big, standard-issue
Black frames, glasses a little like
Plymouths for the face.

This was when summers were all the X-15,
Mickey Mantle and Roberto Clemente,
TV dinners and the drive-in.

Summers had a smell then. When you inhaled
You got the sound of crickets and cicadas
As well in your nose, and *Sputnik* too—

A word that rolled around in our mouths
Then spat itself out. *Sputnik*. We said it
All the time. Things were changing.

IN THE STRONG HOLD OF HER THIN ARMS

My grandmother's hair was long:
Not long like nights filled
With unsettling dreams, which end—
Her hair was longer, like January
Growing to September,
So much was the care she gave
Each turn and fiber and knot as she brushed.
To look at her hair was to look, hair by hair
As she did, separately at each strand,
So that to see it all took two people
Side-by-side looking for days.

In her hair she held the seasons,
The winter of its ends,
The autumn of its middle.
On her head the heat of the sun
And the heat of holding her head up
Made a summer of her struggle:
People standing next to her
After a walk in the desert
Could feel the warmth coming out of her hair.
Animals loved her. They could hide
Forever in her hair as she held them,
Could make their words to her stay
In the secluded world of her embrace.

And underneath, on the underside, the humid
Light rain of water and sweat,
The strong, wide roots of this great hair
River, with its tide and its hundred years:
On this river's currents ran her thoughts,
Each one on a given length of hair—
A thought, or a dream, a worry—
So that her words reached out
Like so many thin arms
And listening to her, when she sang
And when she hummed,
Was to be held.

A September Death

A September death is a quiet one,
Quiet now,
But loud enough in the making.
Outside, the season is changing—
The breath of fall is in the air,
Dusk is in the day.
We can feel them, feel
The light they take with them.
The world is complicit in these ends,
Fall, and dusk, and sleep,
Teaching us through the centuries
Not to be surprised, not scared.
Spring will come, we know it.
But what small consolation against the wind.

A September death is a quiet one,
Even as the life that made it was fire,
Was summer, was heat, was hard.
We are not scared.
Spring will come, we know it.
All of this, what was it
But a diamond being forged?
That hard, that much, even now.
If so, we will wear it,
A gift from the hard season of this life.
It is what is left to us:
Know it to be heart-shaped,
Know it to be a good diamond.

If I Leave You

for Joaquin

Heaven has once again become valuable to me.
Somewhere along, I lost it

And I'm not saying I've found it again.
But I have a son now and he's almost six.

He's the one who needs it.
Or maybe he doesn't.

Six-year-olds do pretty good
Without any help from me.

I guess I'm saying it's me—
I am the one who needs it, but for him.

I need heaven again
So that I've got something to say,

The same way I needed something said to me
About dog heaven

And every other time
There was nothing else to say.

In those moments there's a heaven somewhere
Inside the word itself,

And maybe that's all
There needs to be.

What it is,
Is that there needs to be something.

It's that uncomplicated.
There needs to be something

And I need to be able to say it
When my boy looks at me

And when I look back at him.
I need this word,

And he needs me to have it
When he talks about his grandfather

Or Aunt Connie
Or six-toed Hector the Pal-Cat we had forever.

It's not bigger than that,
And it's not smaller.

It's a nothing jump from there
To guardian angels,

To the picture from my bedroom,
The picture that became part of the wall

After so many years. You know which one:
Two kids crossing a bridge,

High up in some kind of mountains,
The two of them almost ready to fall

Off the rickety planks, and no parents anywhere.
Just the green angel,

Big and happy-eyed and watching them
So that I felt better

Looking at it in the dark
As I got myself ready

To go to sleep,
Wherever Sleep was.

Going to sleep:
It sounded like going somewhere—

Away from home
And by myself—

To the terror I see now
My parents must have harbored

Every time
I started out,

Just the way I feel it when my son lies down.
Just the way

The only thing I can do
For My Little and Good Man

Is pack him a lunch of heaven
For the trail,

Heaven and angels
And gold-talk—something

To carry him along
When I can't be there.

It's all I can do and it isn't much
And it's all that was done for me.

I've got a couple of words for him.
And that's it.

That's all he can carry.

It's nothing to jump further, as well,
To growing up small-town:

Unlocked doors,
And the time I shocked my parents

Because I saw their eyes get so big—
I'll tell you—

When I told them
I wanted to be a priest.

It wasn't true exactly;
It was just the fifties.

I was in catechism.
The space race was on,

And in our nun's classroom
A bulletin board marked attendance

By everybody having a paper spaceship
She moved up one big planet toward God

Each Thursday you came here after school.
I wanted to get to heaven first.

It was a strange goal,
All of us still being alive

And fifth-graders like we were.

I don't know if I believe in heaven.
It's true I need it.

This is a funny thing
To hear myself say.

Maybe that nun was right.
Maybe you needed heaven

Right in the classroom,
And when you are alive

And not just dead.
I can't believe she was right,

And I don't want to.
I don't believe

She gave me the answer to anything else,
Not even what happened

To the ark of the covenant,
Which became my favorite question that year

Because nobody could answer it
Until they made the Indiana Jones movies,

And then all I wanted to say was,
I thought of this plot first.

But wearing a scapular,
Making first Communion, that stuff,

It all just got in the way, finally,
And getting dressed up

In good clothes on Sundays—
And then for anything—

Just made me get sick in my stomach.
I still feel that way, mostly.

I don't know when I really learned
Anything about heaven,

Or if I did learn anything
Not already on a postcard

Or a calendar.
But there you are.

I've got a little boy now,
Just the way I was a little boy,

And I don't know what else to do.

Cups of Frothed Chocolate

Southeast of me on the western horse-country map
My childhood drew wide, a place

Bigger than June together with July—
Here was the eighth ocean. Unnamed,

This Sonoran desert scrub, the creosote,
The cactus, the waves of rock, the hills

Themselves the waves of a small storm,
Always and everywhere, a small

Irritation and squall of the earth.
We rode our boats in this desert, we knew

How: We could see the great
Expanse of water out there

Because the heat made our eyes
Tear—in this way we were always on the ocean.

The trees were like masts.
The distances seen best and only

From there, from the tops of our small ships,
From the tops of the thousand-year-old mulberry tree.

The view was obstructed by the hills, beyond which we knew
The missions were, and the gold, the cow ponds and mining camps—

Ghost towns now, the ghosts
Coppery and silvery and shining,

Their ribs made of cobwebs, their eyes:
The red hourglasses on the stomachs of the spiders.

We came into this ocean world easy,
Cups of frothed chocolate with coconut and pig

Cookies, the long rectangles of fudge.
We kids were made of this world, made from the secret

Minutes of the men tasting
The brandy, the cognac, the waters from other places.

It was a world, in those days, made of simple things:
Lace doilies on the backs of the easy chairs,

Doilies on the sofas, everything neat, something
Like a desire even for doilies on the babies.

Neat and orderly, too, the Elks and the V.F.W.,
Their parades and the park and the drums and bugles,

Those cocked hats—which themselves looked like doilies
On the men, hats heavied down with medals on their sides:

These men carried what they had done on their heads,
The way women in some places carry water jugs.

We couldn't see inside these war-men, our fathers,
We couldn't see what they carried on their heads—

We saw only that they looked like the trees,
Trees whose mulberries hung down like the medals.

The mulberries we knew:
They were blue, sweet and red, their taste

Staying in our mouths, their color
Resonant purple on our hands and on the towels—

Purple but with a little green from somewhere.
Moras they are called in Spanish, *purples,*

Something of a friend to the color of a heart,
To the rootlike vein in a thin leg,

To the color on the top of a palsied hand—
There's an aura there,

Purple like that. Deep in the tongue
Where the West was, the horses,

Our boats in the only ocean we knew,
Our ocean. Deep in the tongue.

THE LEMON KIND OF BASEBALL

Even though I had a six-finger glove
I couldn't stay in Little League
Because I didn't have a ride home.

I played it anyway, a game of our own
That came to the hand
Naturally, in time, a friend

With a hundred names and a thousand rules,
Every summer different from the last
So that the game,

The game was new every time.
At home our game was lighter
And cheaper and tricks.

We took a yellow plastic lemon,
The kind lemon juice comes in.
We stuffed it with rags.

With a match we melted
The open, sticking-out end flat, into a seal—
The way we later imagined dogs got fixed.

Our bats were piñata bats.
We swung them one-handed.
We had to, to be fast. You know how I mean,

The way a plastic lemon full of rags will drop,
Will fly and turn corners in the air
Better than a bird, almost.

That was the thing: the pitch,
The swing and the hit and the run and the air.
That was the thing, Tommy. I remember it

Right now, all of it together in my hands.
I know you do, too.
I know you're out there in your life.

Remember when you were my brother every day?
Don't worry, Tom. It's funny calling you *Tom*.
Don't worry, Tommy. We were good.

DOMINGO LIMÓN

In high school I had a friend
Like you had a friend,
The kind since first grade,

The kind you could count on
Not one way or the other,
Just always to be there,

One more name in the morning,
Somebody we would have missed
The way we would have been missed

If we had not come.
Domingo Limón. Sunday Lemon.
You don't forget a name like that.

Mingo rode his face tractorlike
Down the furrow of years
Our growing up took.

He kept his face to the ground,
He kept his eyes to the ground.
He might have grown taller

If he had looked up.
If he had looked up.
That's all.

After high school he grew the goatee.
We saw what it meant,
Even if we couldn't say.

In that strap of hair
There was a cruel understanding
If one looked hard enough:

The goatee was a simple rudder.
That's what high school gave him.
A way to move.

That was high school on his chin.
That line was all of us.
It was a small map,

A gathering of meridians, braided,
Descriptive of how to stand straight
In the sand and the water and among the rocks.

He could not have spoken
His reasons for growing the goatee,
The same way we could not understand.

But it spoke for itself,
This hair he put first toward the world,
There on a putting-out of his chin.

When he smiled with his teeth
It was the beginning of the voyage each time,
His teeth like ivory thumbs

Hitchhiking themselves toward some adventure,
His teeth the many tusks
Worn off a single elephant

Who would not be stopped,
Who came back to the two holes of the gun,
The two holes of his own nostrils,

Because how else does a rudder lead but straight?
And what a good song of a rudder
That hair below his lip was,

That black thing
That kept him going
But would not let him stop.

It was a rudder and a song both,
And together they made a motor.
Added to his body it let him be a boat,

His white and yellow and brown teeth
Now a mouthful of women at the prow,
These teeth-women facing one another

In the angular, comfortable way they did,
Dancing a *sandunga* of loose conversation,
The hardy rhythm of blue risk.

Those women who were his smile,
They let him move away from the shore.
This smile and the goatee that started him,

They sailed him fully from the shoreline,
That goatee becoming a leg
That pushed him from the dock.

It pushed him far and it took him farther —
But no one knows where.
It was not on our map.

We don't know the death
Toward which a rudder like that eases a boy
Who just looked like a man,

A boy who was after all the elephant,
Not just the ivory.
He was the elephant

And the boat to get us to the elephants,
And the rudder too.
The boy who was everything,

Just small. Nothing loud.
He was the hero
And the story itself, as well,

The way in third grade he said he was,
Though we laughed because we didn't understand
When he talked to himself.

But he was the hero and the story and us.
And all we could do was watch.
He had no words to tell us what he saw.

He knew we could not know.
It was a plow, finally,
That goatee, that blade into the earth.

He knew we could not hold against our lips

The edge of the plow
Steel on the hip-bone

Tearing up everything,
The whole body under it.
I still see it, Mingo.

HOLDING MY SHIRTS

Hunched washerman in the dawdling waters
Bent to a work of days

In a small town—
I know this man.

I know his family
And they know me.

They have a business in washing.
I went to school with this boy.

The man who was that boy has my shirts.
On these days, in this season,

He has me in his hands—
I can tell by his eyes

And he can tell by mine,
I know.

In my shirts—
When I am not in my shirts—

He finds me, something of me
To make the shirts mine.

He finds the form of my arms,
The light smells of my neck.

He sees me with his hands
And with his nose.

He pushes me with his fingers.
He makes me leave from the shirts

But he is not angry.
He returns the shirts to me

Folded. I am embarrassed at his work,
His touching me.

In the fold there is something of him.
I wish there were not.

WRITING FROM MEMORY

My father got up and put on his dress.
It's the fifties and there are stockings,

The kind with lines that go up like a part
In the thick hair of his calf.

He adjusts his bra like anyone,
And we don't think much of it, this morning,

When he misses the catch and asks for help.
He bends over and looks through the closet,

Picking out a right-colored pair of shoes,
Something he knows will be, even in that dimness,

Pale enough to match his purse.
My mother doesn't get up, not right away, not easy,

Making some noise as she lies there,
Rubbing her hand across the thick stubble of her face.

She asks if her brown trousers are clean,
But nobody answers and she shakes her head.

As she gets up she puts a hand inside her underwear,
Rubbing a buttock hard.

She puts on a sleeveless T-shirt,
Then a shoulder holster, but no gun—

Not before breakfast. We've all agreed on that one.
And for God's sake, we say, Mom, brush your teeth.

My sister puts on her jeans, and after zipping up
She moves her thing around, as if anyone cares,

Until she gets it just right, just to the side of the seam.
She keeps leaving the toilet seat up

And walking around the house without a shirt on
To show her pecs off. She flexes one for me,

That little bounce looking like a wink.
Then there's me. The golden boy, the good

Reader. Oh, yeah, I was perfect
Is what I remember.

I would pull on a cotton blouse—
Blue, with a neat, pleated skirt—

Then a sweater. I held my books up to my chest.
It made my parents feel better.

The day started. We were off, to our jobs,
To Coronado Elementary School, to whatever was next.

Finally, we just got in the family car
And drove it straight out of the fifties.

By the end of the century we'd be different people.
We'd be fond of saying, *Those days don't seem real anymore.*

And it's true.
We've forgotten all of this about one another.

Now, when we talk about who we were
We tell some other family's story.

SOME EXTENSIONS ON THE SOVEREIGNTY
OF SCIENCE

for my father

1

When the thought came to him it was so simple he shook his head.
People are always looking for kidneys when their kidneys go bad.

But why wait? Why not look when you're healthy?
If two good kidneys do the trick, wouldn't three do the job even better?

Three kidneys. Maybe two livers. You know. Two hearts, of course.
Instead of repairing damage, why not think ahead?

Why not soup up the car? Why not be a touring eight-cylinder classic,
Or one of those old, sixteen-cylinder, half-mile-long Duesenbergs?

2

The hardest work of the last quarter of the twentieth century is to find
An edge in the middle. When something explodes, for example,

Nobody is confused about what to do—you look toward it.
Loud is a magnet. But the laws of magnetism are more complex.

One might just as well try this: When something explodes,
Turn exactly opposite from it and see what there is to see.

The loud will take care of itself, and everyone will be able to say
What happened in that direction. But who is looking

The other way? Nature, that magician and author of loud sounds,
Zookeeper and cook, electrician and provocateur—

Maybe these events are Nature's sleight of hand, and the real
Thing that's happening is in the other hand,

Or behind or above or below or inside us.

3

On a recent trip to Bloomington, Indiana, I was being driven there
From Indianapolis and my friend pointed out some hills along the way,

Saying that these hills were made as a result of the farthest reach of
The Ice Age glacier. I had been waiting for this moment

Ever since fifth grade. I could hardly contain myself,
Though I'm sure I just said *uh-huh* in the conversation.

I took a small and delicious breath. *So,* I said, slowly,
That's the terminal moraine, huh? There, I'd said it,

The phrase I had saved up since the moment I found it
In that fifth-grade reader: *terminal moraine.*

I had never said it aloud. What's a little scary, of course,
Is that I was more excited about remembering

Than about the hills themselves. But if it was scary, it was sweet
In the mouth, too. In a larger picture, one way or another,

The Ice Age glacier was still a force to be reckoned with.

4

The reason you can't lose weight later on in life is simple enough.
It's because of how so many people you know have died,

And that you carry a little of each of them with you.

5

The smallest muscle in the human body is in the ear.
It is also the only muscle that does not have blood vessels;

It has fluid instead. The reason for this is clear:
The ear is so sensitive that the body, if it heard its own pulse,

Would be devastated by the amplification of its own sound.
In this knowledge I sense a great metaphor,

But I do not want to be hasty in trying to capture or describe it.
Words are our weakest hold on the world.

NOTES

"The Birdman of Nogales": I never knew the Birdman's name, but I can
still see him.

"Kid Hielero": It's true what they say about the connection between
watermelons and people dying. This is not the only time I know of it
happening.

"Common Crows in a Winter Tree": I wrote this poem at Pratt House,
Vassar College.

"Chinese Food in the Fifties": The floor-to-ceiling birdcage in this restau-
rant is not an exaggeration. If you entered too quickly, the birds near
the bottom of the cage would bolt to the top, and a small, wafting aura
of feathers would present itself, particularly in the late afternoon as the
sun came through the blinds just right. I encountered a similar phenom-
enon one other time many years ago, as I was hiking on a summer
afternoon along the arroyo near my house. I found a turn in the creek
that had created a small, rounded section of land overhung by cotton-
wood and mesquite trees. It was the time of year when the white seeds
of the cottonwood filled the air, and as I rounded the bend the experi-
ence took my breath away and has stayed with me for life. I stood
there, the next few minutes simply warm, hazy, watery, blurry, and
perfect.

"Domingo Limón": This is a poem, but it is as well Domingo Limón
himself, a friend of mine since childhood. The untimeliness of his
death was only heightened by a cruel foreshadowing, something out
of a potboiler.

A week before our tenth high school reunion, the local newspaper
reported Domingo Limón's death, though the article was entirely erro-
neous. It came to our attention because one does not forget a name like
his. When we showed up at the reunion, so did he, and there followed
as much laughter as nostalgia.

Not a week after the reunion, however, Domingo suffered a serious
health crisis and, incredibly, he died. No warnings, no prior condition.

ABOUT THE AUTHOR

Alberto Ríos, born in Nogales, Arizona, is the author of eight
books and chapbooks of poetry, three collections of short
stories, and a memoir. His books of poems include *Teodoro
Luna's Two Kisses, The Lime Orchard Woman, The Warrington Poems,
Five Indiscretions,* and *Whispering to Fool the Wind.* His three
collections of short stories are *The Curtain of Trees, Pig Cookies,*
and *The Iguana Killer.* His memoir about growing up on the
Mexico-Arizona border—called *Capirotada*—recently won the
Latino Literary Hall of Fame Award. Ríos is the recipient of the
Arizona Governor's Arts Award, fellowships from the
Guggenheim Foundation and the National Endowment for the
Arts, the Walt Whitman Award, the Western States Book
Award for Fiction, and six Pushcart Prizes in both poetry and
fiction. His work has appeared in over 175 national and interna-
tional literary anthologies and has been adapted to dance and
both classical and popular music. Ríos is presently Regents'
Professor of English at Arizona State University.

The Chinese character for poetry is made up of two parts: "word" and
"temple." It also serves as pressmark for Copper Canyon Press.

Founded in 1972, Copper Canyon Press remains dedicated to
publishing poetry exclusively, from Nobel laureates to new and
emerging authors. The Press thrives with the generous patronage of
readers, writers, booksellers, librarians, teachers, students, and
funders–everyone who shares the conviction that poetry invigorates
the language and sharpens our appreciation of the world.

PUBLISHERS' CIRCLE
Allen Foundation for the Arts
Lannan Foundation
Lila Wallace–Reader's Digest Fund
National Endowment for the Arts

EDITORS' CIRCLE
Thatcher Bailey
Breneman Jaech Foundation
Cynthia Hartwig and Tom Booster
Port Townsend Paper Company
Emily Warn and Daj Oberg
Washington State Arts Commission

FOR INFORMATION AND CATALOGS:
COPPER CANYON PRESS
Post Office Box 271
Port Townsend, Washington 98368
360/385-4925
poetry@coppercanyonpress.org
www.coppercanyonpress.org

This book was designed and typeset by Phil Kovacevich using Quark Xpress 4.1 on a Macintosh G4. The typeface, Perpetua, was designed by Eric Gill in 1925 and first appeared in a limited edition of the book *The Passion of Perpetua and Felicity*. This book was printed by McNaughton & Gunn.